FOR THE LOVE OF SPORTS

ULTIMATE FRISBEE

Linda Hopkins

www.openlightbox.com

Step 1
Go to **www.openlightbox.com**

Step 2
Enter this unique code
PMDVX83YS

Step 3
Explore your interactive eBook!

AV2 is optimized for use on any device

Your interactive eBook comes with...

Contents
Browse a live contents page to easily navigate through resources

Audio
Listen to sections of the book read aloud

Videos
Watch informative video clips

Weblinks
Gain additional information for research

Slideshows
View images and captions

Try This!
Complete activities and hands-on experiments

Key Words
Study vocabulary, and complete a matching word activity

Quizzes
Test your knowledge

Share
Share titles within your Learning Management System (LMS) or Library Circulation System

Citation
Create bibliographical references following APA, CMOS, and MLA styles

This title is part of our AV2 digital subscription

1-Year Grades K–5 Subscription
ISBN 978-1-7911-3320-7

Access hundreds of AV2 titles with our digital subscription.
Sign up for a FREE trial at **www.openlightbox.com/trial**

FOR THE LOVE OF SPORTS

ULTIMATE FRISBEE

CONTENTS

What Is Ultimate Frisbee?

The **frisbee** was invented in 1948 by Walter Frederick Morrison. He was an American inventor. Morrison came up with the idea for this plastic disk after throwing cake tins on the beach with his wife.

In 1968, camp advisor Jared Kass introduced his students to **ultimate** frisbee at a summer camp. He had the idea of playing the game in teams. Kass called it "ultimate" because he thought it was the ultimate sport. While the sport is popularly known as ultimate frisbee, its official name today is simply ultimate.

Ultimate frisbee was first known as "frisbee football."

In 1968, one of the students from Kass's camp, Joel Silver, started an ultimate frisbee team at his school in New Jersey. It began as a joke but became a popular sport. Silver also wrote down the first rules of the game.

Ultimate frisbee is played between two teams of up to seven players. The disk gets passed between teammates. Each team tries to score points by catching the disk in the other team's **end zone**.

It takes skill and practice to correctly throw and catch a frisbee disk.

*The **longest ultimate frisbee marathon** lasted **85 hours** and **1 minute**.*

*Ultimate frisbee is one of the **fastest-growing team sports** in North America.*

*The **longest flying disk throw**, made in **2016**, was **1,108 feet** (338 meters).*

Getting Ready to Play

The main item needed to play a game of ultimate frisbee is the disk itself. Disks come in many different colors and designs. There are no rules about the color of the disk. White is a popular base color because it can be seen well in the day and at night.

Official ultimate disks weigh 6.17 ounces (175 grams), which is a little heavier than a regular frisbee. Their **diameter** is 10.5 inches (27 centimeters).

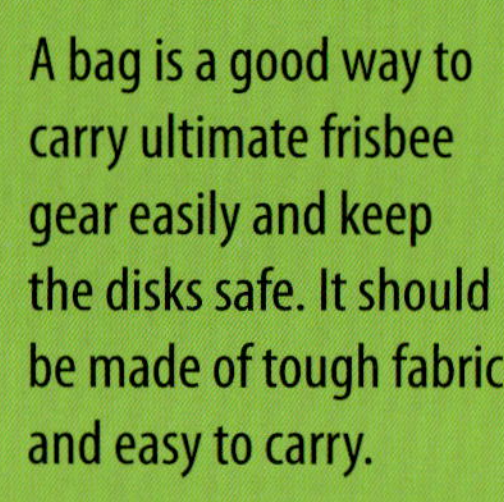

A bag is a good way to carry ultimate frisbee gear easily and keep the disks safe. It should be made of tough fabric and easy to carry.

Players need comfortable shirts made of strong materials that will not rip easily. Shirts must also be breathable to keep players from sweating too much or becoming overheated.

Ultimate frisbee involves a great deal of running and jumping. This makes it important for players to wear the right clothing and shoes. Players often wear gloves, cleats, and comfortable clothes.

Friction gloves help protect players' hands when catching the frisbee. They can be used in wet, cold weather, but also when it is hot.

Players need to be able to move easily. A player's shorts should not be too tight or too loose.

Cleats are shoes that have **studs**. These provide a good grip so that players do not slip. Cleats should be lightweight but strong.

The Ultimate Frisbee Field

An ultimate frisbee field is 120 feet (37 meters) wide and 330 feet (100 m) long. There is an end zone at either end of the field. Players must stay in their end zone until the disk has been thrown.

A brick mark is located on both sides of the field near the center. Each brick mark is 60 feet (18 m) from the end zone. It marks the spot where teams can choose to start from if the disk goes out of bounds.

The field must be flat and clear of **obstacles**. Official ultimate frisbee tournaments are played on real or **synthetic** grass fields. Ultimate frisbee can also be played on the beach or indoors.

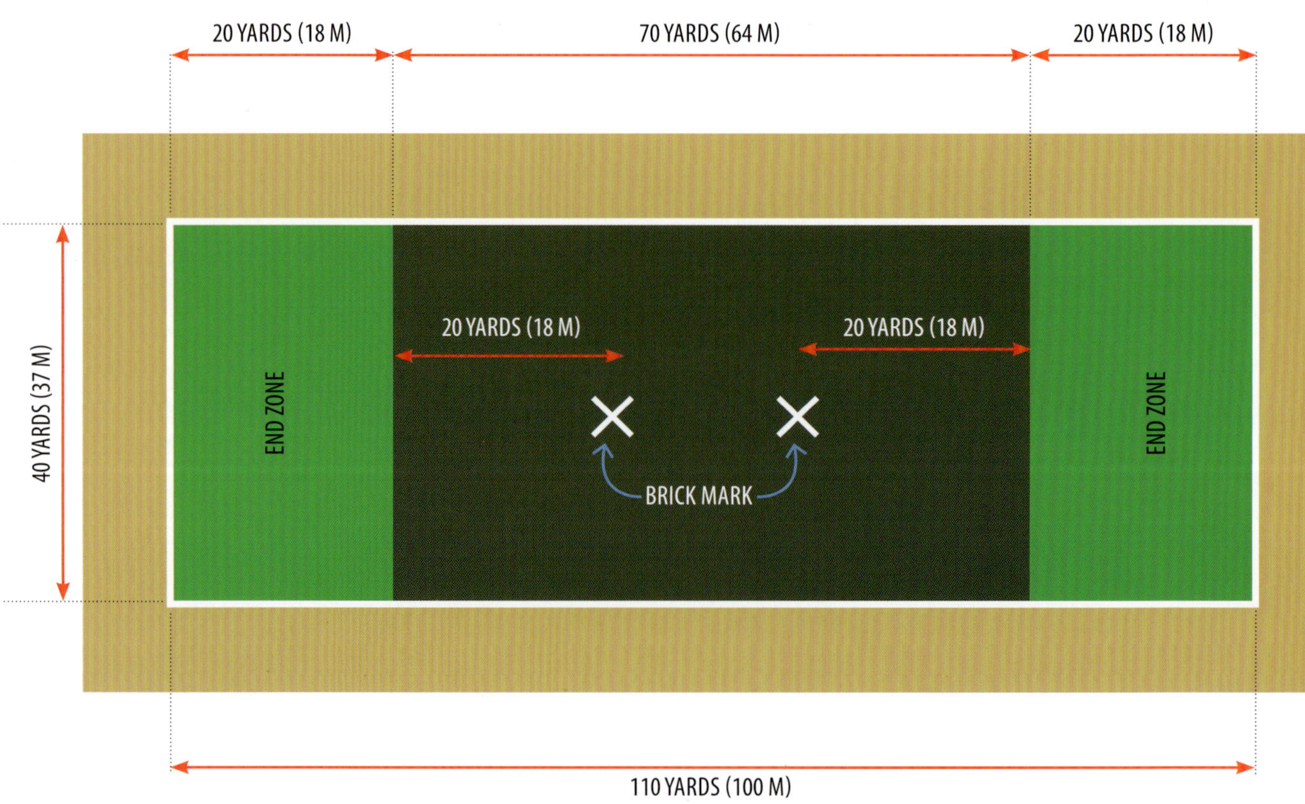

World Ultimate Championships

The World Ultimate Club Championships (WUCC) is held every four years. High-ranking ultimate frisbee clubs can compete in these championships. The tournament has been hosted by different cities around the world, including Perth, Australia, and Lecco, Italy.

Cincinnati, United States

In 2018 and 2022, the World Ultimate Club Championships was held in Cincinnati, Ohio, at the Lebanon Sports Complex. The site has 29 ultimate frisbee fields. In 2022, 128 teams from 30 countries competed there.

Keeping Score

An ultimate frisbee team's goal is to score more points than the **opposing** team. A point is scored whenever the disk is caught by a player in the opposing side's end zone. Both of a player's feet must land in the end zone for the catch to count. If the catch is made with one foot in the end zone and one foot out, it is called straddling. A straddled catch does not count for a point.

Teams switch sides after every point. The team that scored the point starts the next throw. There are many different kinds of throws and catches in ultimate frisbee.

A game is finished when a point cap or time cap is reached. A point cap is usually 15 points, and the winning team must be 2 points ahead. If either team reaches 17 points, the game is over, even if the other team has 16 points.

A pull is a throw that is used to pass the disk to the other team when starting a new play.

A time cap is the maximum length of time that a game can be played. This is usually 100 minutes. If a game reaches 100 minutes, the team with the most points wins, even if it has fewer than 15 points.

There are no referees in ultimate frisbee. Every player is expected to be fair and respect other players. This is called the Spirit of the Game and is a very important part of playing. At the end of each game, the teams score each other on how well they kept the Spirit of the Game.

The backhand throw is the most common throw. A player holds the disk in one hand and twists to the other side, then swings out and lets the disk go.

The flick throw takes practice. A player holds the disk between the thumb and forefingers, pulls back the wrist, and flicks the disk forward.

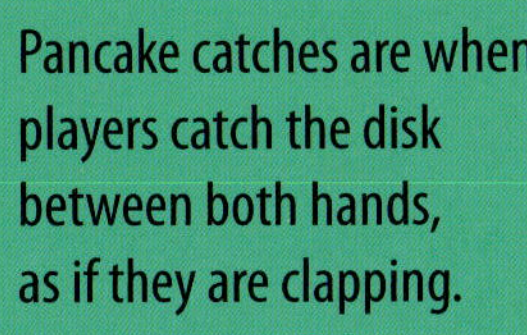

Pancake catches are when players catch the disk between both hands, as if they are clapping.

Rules of the Game

Before a game of ultimate frisbee starts, the team captains will flip one or two disks. This is similar to a coin toss. When one disk is flipped, one of the captains calls "up" or "down." If two discs are flipped, he or she calls "same" or "different." The winner of the flip decides who will throw first. The team that is throwing the disk is the offense. The other team is the defense.

To start a game, each team lines up at its end zone. One of the players on the defense will raise a hand to show that his or her team is ready to start playing. Once the disk is thrown, the players can leave the end zone and move around the field.

If a team throws the disk out of bounds, the other team can "brick." This means they can take the disk to their brick mark to carry on playing. Players are not allowed to run with the disk. They can change direction by keeping one foot on the ground and moving the other foot in a different direction. This is called a **pivot**.

The person holding the disk is the thrower. He or she will throw the disk to a teammate.

In ultimate frisbee, players call their own **fouls**. If a player thinks that the frisbee went out of bounds, the player closest makes the call. Players are not allowed to touch other players.

If the disk touches the ground, it goes to the other team. This is called a turnover.

TURNOVER

Players are out of bounds if they catch the disk outside of the lines.

Playing the Game

Ultimate frisbee has become a popular game all around the world. Every day, millions of people play just for the fun of the game and to enjoy its team spirit. All that they need is a disk, an open field, and enough people to make up two teams.

Ultimate frisbee is also played at the professional level. Within the United States, the game is governed by USA Ultimate. The World Flying Disk Federation (WFDF) is the organization that **governs** ultimate frisbee around the world.

USA Ultimate runs ultimate frisbee camps for children aged 7 to 15 across the United States.

With a focus on the Spirit of the Game, ultimate frisbee teaches players good sportsmanship.

Ultimate Frisbee Championships are held all over the world. International events are organized by the WFDF. One of the largest tournaments is the World Ultimate and Guts Championship (WUGC).

At the WUGC, teams play for their countries instead of their clubs. There are three divisions. These are men's, women's, and mixed divisions.

Other WFDF events are the World Masters Ultimate Club Championship, the World Ultimate Club Championships, the World Beach Ultimate Championship, and the World Junior Ultimate Championship. Each of these championships also has men's, women's, and mixed divisions.

There are more than 800 college ultimate frisbee teams in the United States.

Every year, more than 15,000 players compete in the USA Ultimate Club Championships.

History of Ultimate Frisbee

Before the invention of the plastic frisbee, people threw pie tins and cake pans. The name “frisbee” comes from the Frisbie Pie Company, which was started in 1871. It made pies that were baked in metal tins. Workers at the company began throwing tins to each other during lunch breaks. It did not take long before students from Yale University nearby caught on to the new game. Soon Frisbie pie tins were being thrown around the Yale campus.

The Ultimate Players Association (UPA) was formed in 1979. The first UPA Nationals were played in State College, Pennsylvania, that year.

1968 The first official game of ultimate frisbee is played at Columbia High School in Maplewood, New Jersey.

1970 Joel Silver, Buzzy Hellring, and Jon Hines, three students at Columbia High School, write the first set of rules for ultimate frisbee.

1980 The first Ultimate European Championship is played in Paris, France, and is won by Finland.

1984 The World Flying Disk Federation is formed.

2015 The International Olympic Committee (IOC) officially recognizes the WFDF. This means that ultimate frisbee could eventually become an Olympic sport.

2022 The United States defends its mixed team ultimate title at the World Games, held in Birmingham, Alabama.

*The **first organized ultimate frisbee tournament** was played in **1975**. Eight teams took part.*

1975

*The **Club Women's Division** launched in **1981**. Club ultimate is the **highest level** of ultimate frisbee teams.*

*In **1964**, the **first Professional Model Frisbee** was introduced by the toy company **Wham-O**.*

Superstars of Ultimate Frisbee

Stars of ultimate frisbee have inspired many new players.

Suzanne Fields

BIRTH DATE: September 1, 1953
HOMETOWN: Haiku, United States

CAREER FACTS:

- Fields organized the Women's Division of the UPA. She was the first Women's Director, a position she held from 1981 to 1984.
- Fields organized and captained the U.S. women's team, Melting Pot. The team won the first World Ultimate Championships in Gothenburg, Sweden, in 1983.
- In 1990, Fields competed at the WUGC in Oslo, Norway, as part of the first U.S. mixed team. The team won first place.

Tom "TK" Kennedy

BIRTH DATE: March 31, 1949
HOMETOWN: Santa Barbara, United States

CAREER FACTS:

- Kennedy founded and captained the Santa Barbara Condors.
- He led the Santa Barbara Condors to victory in the 1977 USA Ultimate National Championships.
- Kennedy was the first National Director of the UPA. He held the position from 1979 to 1982.
- Along with Irv Kalb, Kennedy co-authored the book *Ultimate: Fundamentals of the Sport*.

Kelly Green

BIRTH DATE: August 25, 1960
HOMETOWN: Paso Robles, United States

CAREER FACTS:

- Green played with the Lady Condors in California, winning five national championships with her team.
- The Lady Condors also won a world championship during Green's tenure.
- Green started and coached the Michigan State Women's Ultimate Team.
- She also coached the Women's College Team at the University of California, Santa Barbara.

Patrick van der Valk

BIRTH DATE: 1964
HOMETOWN: The Hague, The Netherlands

CAREER FACTS:

- Van der Valk is often called the "King of Beach Ultimate." He is largely responsible for making beach ultimate more popular around the world.
- Van der Valk helped to start the Beach Ultimate Lovers Association (BULA) in 2001 and was its first Executive Director.
- In 2004, van der Valk and BULA organized the first World Beach Ultimate Championships in Figueira de Foz, Portugal.

Beau Kittredge

BIRTH DATE: June 23, 1982
HOMETOWN: Fairbanks, United States

CAREER FACTS:

- Kittredge is considered one of ultimate frisbee's best players. He became famous for jumping over another player in 2006.
- Kittredge has won gold in seven world championships.
- He has also won six gold medals and three silver medals at the USA Ultimate National Championships.
- Kittredge was named American Ultimate Disk League's (AUDL's) Most Valuable Player (MVP) twice in a row, in 2014 and 2015.

Leslie Calder

BIRTH DATE: October 13, 1970
HOMETOWN: Vancouver, Canada

CAREER FACTS:

- Between 1994 and 2007, Calder won seven Canadian Championships.
- Calder was the captain for Team Canada at the WUGC in 2000, leading them to win gold.
- She won another gold medal with Team Canada at the WUGC in 2004.
- Calder was inducted into the Canadian Hall of Fame in 2013 and into the U.S. Ultimate Hall of Fame in 2017.

Rowan McDonnell

BIRTH DATE: June 1, 1989
HOMETOWN: East Lyme, United States

CAREER FACTS:

- McDonnell is considered one of the most **versatile** players in the game of ultimate frisbee.
- In 2018, McDonnell received the AUDL MVP award and was named the Ultiworld Offensive Player of the Year.
- He was named the Ultiworld Player of the Year in 2022.
- McDonnell has coached more than 25 ultimate frisbee programs. In 2017, he founded the American Ultimate Academy, which runs camps and programs that teach children how to play ultimate frisbee.

Staying Healthy

Healthy eating is an important part of any sport, including ultimate frisbee. Players should have a healthy diet that includes fruits, vegetables, grains, and protein. Protein comes from meat, fish, nuts, and eggs. It builds muscle and helps the body to recover from injury. Sugary snacks, such as candy bars and soda, are not considered healthy. They do not have most of the **nutrients** that players need.

It is also very important for players to drink plenty of water. Athletes lose water when they sweat, and it needs to be replaced. Players should drink water before, during, and after a game.

Lifting weights strengthens an athlete's arm muscles.

Calcium, which is found in dairy products, such as milk, yogurt, and cheese, is needed to build strong bones.

Ultimate frisbee is a fast, high-energy game. Players can injure their knees and ankles while running and jumping. Sometimes, players also dive to catch the disk and may be hurt as they hit the ground.

To avoid injuries, players usually warm up by stretching before each game. They may also strengthen their legs with leg exercises. Players should practice landing with slightly bent knees.

Wearing the right shoes can help prevent injuries caused by slipping and skidding.

THE ULTIMATE FRISBEE QUIZ

- 1 -

Who **invented** the **frisbee**?

- 2 -

What kind of **shoes** should an ultimate **frisbee player wear**?

- 3 -

How long is an **ultimate frisbee field**?

- 4 -

How often are the **World Ultimate Club Championships** held?

- 5 -

What is a **pancake catch**?

- 6 -

How many **players** make up an ultimate frisbee **team**?

- 7 -

What is the **name of the organization** that governs ultimate frisbee around the world?

- 8 -

In what year was the **Ultimate Players Association** formed?

- 9 -

Who is known as the **"King of Beach Ultimate"**?

- 10 -

In which city was the **2022 World Ultimate Club Championships** held?

ANSWERS: 1 Walter Frederick Morrison 2 Cleats 3 330 feet (100 m) (110 yards) 4 Every four years 5 When players catch the disk between both hands, as if they are clapping 6 Up to seven 7 World Flying Disk Federation (WFDF) 8 1979 9 Patrick van der Valk 10 Cincinnati, Ohio

Key Words

diameter: the distance from one point on the edge of a circle, through the circle's center, to the point on the opposite side

end zone: an area at the end of a playing field

fouls: actions that are against the rules of a sport

frisbee: a disk made of plastic that people throw and catch as part of a game

governs: controls, directs, or strongly influences the actions and conduct of something

nutrients: the substances in food that the body processes to enable it to function

obstacles: objects that block someone's way

opposing: competing or fighting against each other

pivot: turn or twist

studs: small pieces of metal, plastic, or rubber that project from a surface, such as the sole of a shoe

synthetic: made by people, often as a copy of something natural

ultimate: best or greatest of its kind

versatile: able to do many different things

Index

Get the best of both worlds.

AV2 bridges the gap between print and digital.

The expandable resources toolbar enables quick access to content including **videos**, **audio**, **activities**, **weblinks**, **slideshows**, **quizzes**, and **key words**.

Animated videos make static images come alive.

Resource icons on each page help readers to further **explore key concepts**.

Published by Lightbox Learning Inc.
276 5th Avenue, Suite 704 #917
New York, NY 10001
Website: www.openlightbox.com

Library of Congress Cataloging-in-Publication Data

Names: Hopkins, Linda, author.
Title: Ultimate Frisbee / Linda Hopkins.
Description: New York, NY : Lightbox Learning Inc., 2023. | Series: For the love of sports | Includes index. | Audience: Grades 4-6
Identifiers: LCCN 2022011962 (print) | LCCN 2022011963 (ebook) | ISBN 9781791146078 (library binding) | ISBN 9781791146085 (paperback) | ISBN 9781791146092
Subjects: LCSH: Ultimate (Game)--Juvenile literature.
Classification: LCC GV1097.U48 H67 2023 (print) | LCC GV1097.U48 (ebook) | DDC 796.2--dc23/eng/20220411
LC record available at https://lccn.loc.gov/2022011962
LC ebook record available at https://lccn.loc.gov/2022011963

Printed in Guangzhou, China
1 2 3 4 5 6 7 8 9 0 26 25 24 23 22

122022
101121

Project Coordinator Priyanka Das
Art Director Terry Paulhus
Layout Jean Faye Marie Rodriguez

Photo Credits
Every reasonable effort has been made to trace ownership and to obtain permission to reprint copyright material. The publisher would be pleased to have any errors or omissions brought to its attention so that they may be corrected in subsequent printings.
The publisher acknowledges Alamy, Dreamstime, Getty Images, Shutterstock, and Wikimedia as its primary image suppliers for this title.